MOODS OF
KILVERT
COUNTRY

MOODS OF
KILVERT
COUNTRY

NICK JENKINS & KEVIN THOMAS

HALSGROVE

First published in Great Britain in 2006

Copyright: text and photographs © 2006 Nick Jenkins and Kevin Thomas

Cover photographs – Front: *A view of the Black Mountains.*
Back: *A common scene in the pastures near Hay on Wye.*

Title page photograph: *A detail from the village of Clyro, where Kilvert spent his formative years as curate.*

British Library Cataloguing-in-Publication Data
A CIP record for this title is available from the British Library

ISBN 1 84114 525 4
ISBN 978 1 84114 525 9

HALSGROVE
Halsgrove House
Lower Moor Way
Tiverton, Devon EX16 6SS
Tel: 01884 243242
Fax: 01884 243325
email: sales@halsgrove.com
website: www.halsgrove.com

Printed and bound by D'Auria Industrie Grafiche Spa, Italy

FOREWORD

Wales has always drawn visitors attracted by the magnificence of the peaks of Snowdonia, the grandeur of the Brecon Beacons, the rugged coastline of Pembrokeshire or the rolling pastures and water meadows of the border counties in the east. Even though rapid industrialisation made its mark, the beauty of the Welsh landscape has endured.

Many artists, writers and photographers documented Wales and provided inspiration for those who have followed their journeys. J.M.W. Turner visited on numerous occasions and recorded scenes throughout the country. George Borrow described a 'Wild' Wales in his writings and many others have sought out their locations in order to recapture the sense of timelessness represented in their work.

Francis Kilvert is famous for having kept a diary of the time he spent in Radnorshire and Herefordshire during the 1870s, both as the curate at Clyro and latterly as the vicar at Bredwardine. Though many have read his work as a detailed documentary of the people of the area and an insight into rural life, it is important not to overlook the eloquence of his descriptions of the landscape. The context in which he places the characters is also crucial to the understanding of contemporary rural life.

Society was hierarchical and Kilvert was well aware of this, relying on financial support from landowners and tenant farmers, but at the same time having to provide spiritual support to all his parishioners. No doubt he experienced many events that affected him emotionally, which is possibly why he spent so much time walking alone in the countryside he loved so dearly.

It is in these brief passages from his diary entries that Kevin Thomas and Nick Jenkins have found inspiration for their representations of the landscapes. There are no distinct boundaries to 'Kilvert Country', and they have sought to use the diary as their road map to identify locations that would have been familiar to him. Many places have altered; others have changed little, if at all.

Share with them, as we have shared with Francis Kilvert, the splendour of a landscape largely unscathed by the passage of time and preserved in the pages of Kilvert's Diary, and now in their photographs.

Technical Details

We have always subscribed to the view that it is the person who sees a photograph, and that the camera is merely the tool with which it was taken; if you like, the hardware between the brain and the image. Nevertheless, some people find it both informative and instructive to have an idea of the equipment used. All the images in the book were taken using the following:

Canon D60 digital with a range of focal length lenses from 17mm to 300mm
Nikon F3 with a range of focal length lenses from 17mm to 400mm
Hasselblad 500 CM with a range of focal length lenses from 50mm to 150mm as well as a Hasselblad
 SWC 901 38mm
Nikon F90X Pro with a range of lenses from 28mm to 300mm
Mamiya 645 Pro with 45mm, 80mm and 150mm lenses
Film stock used was Fuji Velvia 50 ASA and Fuji Provia 100 ASA

Kevin Thomas &
Nick Jenkins

Acknowledgements

The authors would like to acknowledge the support and enthusiasm of the Kilvert Society while they were compiling the images selected for this book. In addition we would like to extend our thanks to all those who helped us bring the project to fruition.

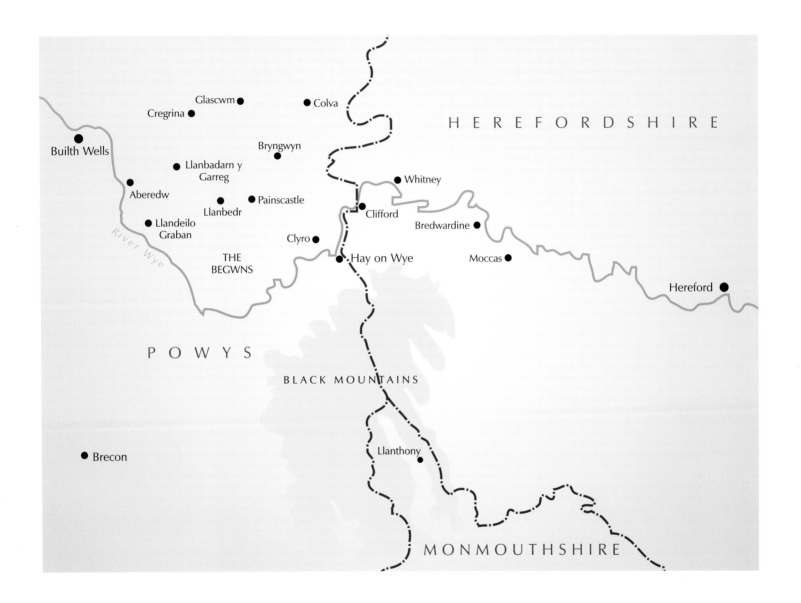

Grouse shooting butts alongside a remote pool deep in the Radnorshire Hills above Painscastle.

Opposite: The clear water of Llan Bwch-llyn Lake

The Parish Church of St Mary, Newchurch. It is here that little Emmeline, who was known to Kilvert, is buried.

An old signpost at Dolleycanney shows the adverse effect of the elements.

Ancient oaks at Moccas Park, referred to by Kilvert as 'the old grey men of Moccas'.

Opposite: Twm Tobacco's grave in the Radnorshire Hills above Llanbedr. Old Twm is thought to have been a packhorse trader, whose remains were discovered up on the ridgeway where he is now buried.

Some original features remain on this farm building at Painscastle.

Opposite: Mountain ponies can be seen feeding in the undulating hills above Painscastle, where Kilvert often walked.

A quiet pool in the Radnorshire Hills,
near Twm Tobacco's grave.

Catkins add a delicate splash of colour to the springtime hedgerows in the Edw Valley.

The bridge over the River Edw, near Llanbadarn y Garreg.

A glimpse of the Wye from Cwmpelved Green.

Opposite: Corn stubble left after harvesting near Clifford.

A small brook cuts a path through the bracken near Llandeilo Graban.

A detail from St Peter's Church, Llanbedr, typical of the style of many
of the little churches to be found in Radnorshire.

Detail of the bridge at Bredwardine, showing the
skills of the bricklayer.

Opposite: The elegant six-arched brick bridge at
Bredwardine was built in 1759.

The porch at
Bredwardine Church.

*I was unaware of the features of the
church at Bredwardine which Kilvert
knew and loved, and had visited on
numerous occasions before reading
about it in the Diary. Having now
made the journey many more times
and at all seasons of the year, we
have seen the carpet of snowdrops,
the spring daffodils, the glorious
summer greenery and the glowing
autumn colours. It has been difficult
to choose our favourite photographs
so here is a selection.* (**KT**)

A carpet of snowdrops in Bredwardine churchyard.

Bredwardine Vicarage, where Kilvert spent his last years.

The elegant setting of Old Court, Bredwardine.

The Parish Church of St Andrew, Bredwardine.

Post box at Brobury. Note the small size of the aperture.

Opposite: Colour changes gradually in early autumn at Bredwardine.

St David's Church, Colva

My first visit to St David's was on a bitterly cold February morning at the beginning of this project. Kilvert described how he had walked across the hills on a warm February day in 1870. How different was my view in the chilling, icy rain as I left the warmth of the car and failed to find inspiration! My second visit was a more pleasant day in May and, though the grass was long and wet and the daffodils past their best, I was able to take some satisfactory photographs in the graveyard. Each time I've been there, I have failed to test the echo from the belfry that Kilvert had been told of by Richard Meredith. Maybe next time... **(KT)**

A gravestone at Colva, surrounded by snowdrops.

An old carved stone county boundary marker near Hay on Wye.

Opposite: An isolated barn on Colva Hill, standing in a warm pool of winter sunshine.

An ornate, decorative cockerel surmounting the lamp post in Llanbedr churchyard.

A finial on the east end of the roof of St David's Church, Glascwm.

The weathervane at Llandeilo Graban Church.

The view from Maesyronnen – probably one of the most idyllic locations in the landscape of Kilvert Country. The place itself is delightful, but the views to the south across the Wye towards the Black Mountains can be breathtaking at any time.

The distant Black Mountains viewed from the Begwn Hills.

Who can fail to be impressed by the grandeur of the Black Mountains, particularly when they are lit either by the early morning sunrise or the late setting sun when viewed against a backdrop of gathering storm clouds?

Views of Maesyronnen Chapel.

Opposite: Maesyronnen Chapel, one of the earliest chapels in the county of Powys.

The lych-gate and tower, St Peter and St Paul Church, Whitney.

The lovely old lych-gate at St Mary's Church, Monnington on Wye.

The gate to the Methodist Chapel, Painscastle. Kilvert seemed to draw little distinction between church and chapel during his visits.

Methodist chapel buildings at Painscastle.

A farmhouse in the centre of Painscastle.

Opposite: View from castle mound, Painscastle.

Victorian post box in Painscastle.

Crossroads – Painscastle.

On one visit I was fascinated to find myself talking to a lady from London who had been billeted, as a child evacuee, at a cottage in the village during the Second World War. **(NJ)**

Methodist Chapel – Painscastle.

Sign at Painscastle Congregational Chapel.

Painscastle Congregational Chapel.
It is odd that Painscastle has two
chapels and no church.

Welsh poppies on the steps of Painscastle Congregational Chapel.

Opposite: Painscastle is a fascinating and historic village, referred to often in the *Diary*. The castle on its grassy mound must have been an imposing sight in Norman times, and the village was probably an important watering hole and stopping point for drovers herding their stock from west Wales to the markets across the border in England. Of course, Kilvert walked there on many occasions during his lengthy excursions into the countryside. One wonders if he would have opted for a car, even if one had been available at the time.

Atmospheric skies over a lake in the Begwn Hills.

Another view from the lake in the Begwn Hills. These hills are in the keeping
of the National Trust, and offer superb views across to the Black Mountains.

The north-facing slope of the Begwns in winter.

A fallen bough from one of the numerous ancient trees found across the area.

Church of St Cewydd, Aberedw. This particular church was one of Kilvert's firm favourites. The view is from the remains of Aberedw Castle.

Stained glass window in St Cewydd's Church, Aberedw.

St CEWYDD

To the GLORY of GOD and to the belo ved memory of WILLIAM THOMAS REES of PONTSHONI, ABEREDW, who died at PENDARREN CRICKHOWELL.

St TEILO

on August 18º 1923, Aged 74 years. "The memory of the Just is Blessed". Erected by his daughter A.NORAH I., FESTING.

Bryngwyn Church porch. Kilvert tells an occasional sad tale of how hard life could be for his parishioners. On a visit to Bryngwyn, Kilvert relates how he meets Tom Gore repairing a stone wall. He has only one pair of shoes and works hard to make a living for himself and his second wife. His first wife had died and so had his four small children, who are buried in a row in the churchyard.

The elegant and rather imposing vicarage at Bryngwyn.

Rich foliage surrounds much of Llangorse Lake.

Opposite: Kilvert and his brother Perch would often hire a boat and go fishing on Llangorse Lake.

The Baskerville Arms in Clyro was known as the Swan Inn during Kilvert's time in the village. It is often mentioned in the *Diary*, though not necessarily in a favourable light. From 1865 to 1872 he lived just across the road in what is now Ashbrook House, and was often disturbed late at night by the drunken revelry that went on. His tolerance for such behaviour seems to have been limited.

Springtime in a lane in the Edw Valley.

Capel y Ffin church (opposite) and church sign.

It wasn't until I visited the small whitewashed church at Capel y Ffin, built in 1762 and dedicated to St Mary, that I could appreciate why Kilvert had described it as resembling an owl. The south porch, which was added in 1817, is as sharp as a beak, the windows are like blinking eyes, and the little bell turret gives the impression of a single ear, cocked to catch the slightest sound of a careless vole or shrew that might pass and provide a nocturnal meal. **(NJ)**

The tiny hamlet of Capel y Ffin.

Ashbrook House was known as Ty Dulas when Kilvert lodged. During the seven years he stayed there (1865–72), he often sat writing near a window and described in some detail what he saw. The weather conditions would change the appearance of the landscape, as they still do. The people fascinated him so much, going about their daily lives, whether working in the fields or simply passing by on their way to Brecon to the west or Hereford to the east.

Llanthony Priory in the Vale of Ewyas.

I wonder what Kilvert would have made of a well-equipped photographer with tripod, case, lenses, filters and exposure meter standing among the grey pointed arches rising from the close cut green turf? He was horrified at the sight of tourists pointing sticks and describing points of interest in the ruins. If he felt they debased the glory of the surroundings, what would he have thought today? **(NJ)**

Opposite: Llanthony Priory is always a haven of peace and tranquillity.

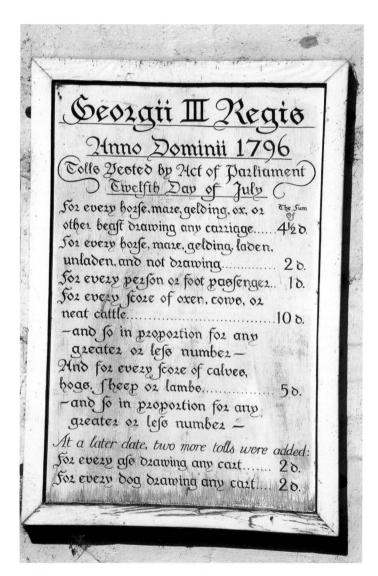

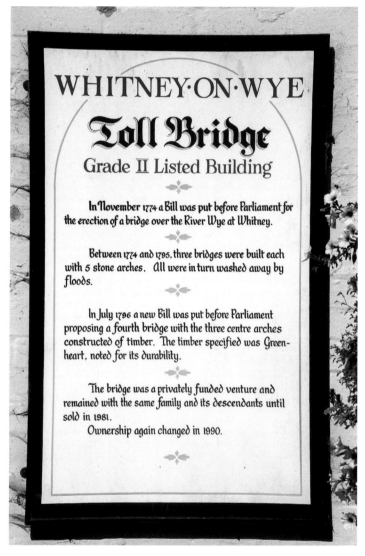

Toll bridge sign, Whitney. The toll bridge as we see it today has spanned the River Wye since the early nineteenth century.

Toll bridge sign, Whitney.

Toll Bridge Cottage, Whitney.

Toll bridge deck, Whitney.

The gravestone of the Rev. John Price in Llanbedr Painscastle Church. Rev. Price was known to Kilvert as 'The Solitary.'

Church of St Peter, Llanbedr Painscastle.

River Edw at Aberedw, so beloved of Kilvert.

Llanstephan suspension bridge
over the River Wye near Llyswen.

We think of the River Wye as a grand river, but it has many hidden little gems like this detail of the riverbank near Otter's Pool.

Narrow lanes with high-sided hedgerows dissect the rolling, patchwork countryside. They are filled with the scent of wild roses, honeysuckle and freshly-mown fields in summer, and the richness of wild fruits and the sounds of feeding birds as they prepare for the onset of winter in the autumn.

First signs of spring near Llanbedr.

Opposite: A snowy lane near Llandeilo Graban.

Looking north from the hills above Llan Bwch-llyn.

Opposite: Winter on Llanbedr Hill.

A bleak winter scene above Llandeilo Graban.

Kilvert often mentions the harshness of winter in Radnorshire.

The towering arches of Llanthony
Priory in the Vale of Ewyas.

How often does Kilvert mention the wild flowers to be found in the hedgerows which border the fields and meadows of the area? He lists the varieties in a rich nosegay when describing a meeting with Miss Sandell and the Morrell children on their way home from a ramble on a Saturday in May 1871.

A detail of the door of St Padarn's Church, Llanbadarn y Garreg.

Opposite: St Padarn's Church, Llanbadarn y Garreg. The church is almost certainly medieval
in origin and when we visited, it was sadly in need of a fresh coat of whitewash.

A pastoral scene near Merbach Hill.

Spring lambs and their mothers in rich green pastures.

Lichen and moss on a stone wall: so typical of south Radnorshire.

*Opposite: Coming off the Begwn Hills late one winter afternoon,
I noticed this stand of pines silhouetted against a turbulent sky.
The simplicity of the composition adds to the drama of the
scene, and shows the element of stark winter landscape,
to which Kilvert often referred.* **(KT)**

St David's Church, Rhulen. This beautiful and secluded little church is
claimed to be one of the oldest in Radnorshire.

Opposite: River Wye near Aberedw. At one time Kilvert would have travelled
this stretch by train, long before the closure of the line in the 1960s.

TO THE GLORY OF GOD
AND IN PROUD AND HONOURED
MEMORY OF
CAPT RALPH HOPTON BASKERVILLE,
CORPL WILLIAM C ROBERTS,
PTE FRANCIS H ANTHONY,
" " WILLIAM F FRY,
" " ALBERT HARRIS,
" " JOHN S MEREDITH,
" " JASPER H MOUNTFORD,
" " WILLIAM MORGAN,
" " THOMAS WARNER.
WHO GAVE THEIR LIVES IN THE GREAT WAR
1914 — 1919.

St Michael's Church, Clyro.

96

Interior – St Michael's Church, Clyro, where
Francis Kilvert served as curate from 1865 –1872. It is
interesting to note that the tower as we see it today
was, in fact, built after Kilvert's time.

Interior of St Michaels' Church, Clyro.

The quaint little Post Office and village stores in Clyro.

These pretty seventeenth-century cottages at Clyro probably looked much the same in Kilvert's day. Standing at the east gate of the church, one can imagine him chatting to the parishioners, who were such a significant part of his life during his curacy here.

Victorian letterbox at Hay on Wye.

Postbox outside St Teilo's Church, Llandeilo Graban.

Opposite: Letterbox in the wall of Capel y Ffin Church.

Local natural building materials are used extensively in the architecture of the area.

Opposite: A common scene in the pastures near Hay on Wye

Llanddewi Fach – a tiny church visited by Kilvert and only accessible on foot.

Bridge Cottage, Bredwardine.

The tomb of Father Ignatius in the
ruins of Llanthony Abbey.

*Visited by Kilvert, this 'self appointed' monk
dedicated his entire life to building the abbey,
a task which he never completed. Whenever I
visit this spot, I feel I am being watched.* **(NJ)**

Statue of the Virgin Mary at Llanthony Abbey.

The vicarage at Clifford.

Llanbedr Church after a light snowfall.

Hay Castle stands high above the surrounding buildings of the town of
Hay on Wye – the second-hand bookshop capital of the world.

Opposite: Poplars at sunset near Hay on Wye.

Detail of a front door in Hay on Wye.

Opposite: One of the many streets of Hay on Wye which bustle in summer
and especially during the world famous Hay Book Festival.

A solitary oak tree standing near
Maesyronnen Chapel.

A canoeist enjoys the Wye at Whitney toll bridge.

Well-manicured farmland near Hay on Wye.

A post van delivering the morning mail in the Edw Valley.

Snowdrops and a telephone box
at Llandeilo Graban.

A newly-laid willow hedge near Llanbedr.

The acid yellow of the flower heads of oil seed rape on
gently undulating hills south of the meandering Wye.

St Michael's Church at Moccas, a corruption from old Welsh 'moch gors', meaning 'the common of the pigs'.

Opposite: King Arthur's Stone – a prehistoric cromlech above Dorstone.

Moccas Court, built in 1775 by Anthony Keck.

The magnificent gardens at Moccas Court are a pleasure to visit.

The Vicarage among the trees below the bridge at Bredwardine.

Horses feeding below Clifford Castle.

Opposite: Patchwork fields near Merbach Hill. A typical rural scene in this rolling countryside.

Sheep taking shelter from the afternoon sun at Capel y Ffin.

Another of Kilvert's 'old grey gentlemen' in Moccas Park.

Though many things remain unchanged in the landscape described by Kilvert, obvious changes in agricultural technology have left their mark here and there. Some things change little over time and it is encouraging to see remnants of the use of natural materials and traditional methods still surviving. **(KT)**

Opposite: The soil adds another colour to the landscape so familiar to Kilvert. The rich redness is enhanced when it has been raining. The contrasting light and shadow of the deep furrows after ploughing and planting adds a further dimension to this essentially agricultural landscape.

A tranquil scene below the Bage.

The view towards the Black Mountains from near Llowes.

A red and white Hereford cow at Moccas, amply emphasising the rural and agricultural nature of the county.

Oaks above the River Wye in fields near Maesyronnen.

An old farm near Maesyronnen Chapel.

Every step in the lanes is accompanied by the wide range of wild
flowers, which would have been present in Kilvert's time.

Opposite: Winding lanes contrast with the regimental field lines near Llanbedr.

Detail of the barn at Cwmpelved, typical of
the style seen all over Radnorshire.

Opposite: All that remains of the old Barn at Cwmpelved, so
often visited by Kilvert when out meeting his parishioners.

Towards the Black Mountains from below Bryngwyn.